PRISONER (
My Horrendo
1945

by

Flt. Lt. Phillip Henry Clews ex-RAF.

Dedicated to my wife
Jessie Clews.

Donations will be made by Mrs Clews
from the sale of this book
to
The Dialysis Unit
Kings Mill Hospital
Sutton-in-Ashfield
Nottinghamshire.

Cover photographs:
Top: Boston Stump – the largest Parish Church in Great Britain used for navigation by air crews in World War II.

Middle: Illustration of a Handley Page Halifax bomber.

Bottom: Flt. Lt. Philip Henry Clews.

PRISONER OF WAR
My Horrendous March
1945

by

Flt. Lt. Philip Henry Clews ex-RAF.

Compiled and first published in Great Britain
in March 2004 by Stanley Naylor.

Copyright © Stanley Naylor 2004.

British Library Cataloguing in Publication Data.

ISBN 0-9527846-7-X

All rights reserved. No part of this publication may be reproduced, stored in a retrieval system or transmitted in any form or by any means, electronic, mechanical, photocopying, recorded or otherwise, without prior permission in writing from the publisher. The information is from the author and publishers own knowledge and sources believed to be reliable, but accuracy cannot be guaranteed.

Printed by:
Guardian Press (Boston) Ltd
Nelson Way
Boston
Lincolnshire, PE21 8TS
United Kingdom.

CONTENTS

Introduction -- 4 -5 - 6 - 7

Poem: Home Run - John R. Walsh ---------------------------- 8

Poem: Stand Those Three Towers - Victor Cavendish -- 9 - 10

Royal Air Forces Dedication ------------------------------- 10

Prisoner of War by Philip Clews --------------------------- 11 to 35

Words from Pericles' Funeral Oration ---------------------- 35

Layout of Halifax Navigators Station ---------------------- 36 - 37

Poem: Beyond The Wire - John R. Walsh --------------------- 38 - 39

Poem: Johnny – John R. Walsh ------------------------------ 39

The Handley Page Halifax ---------------------------------- 40

578 RAF Squadron -- 41

Abbreviations --- 42 – 43 - 44

Poem: Remember - John R. Walsh ---------------------------- 44

Acknowledgements -- 45

The Royal British Legion Act of Homage. ------------------- 45

Books written and published by Stanley Naylor. ------------ 46 - 47

(iii)

INTRODUCTION

Although I was in France and Germany from September 1944 to January 1946 with 2831 Squadron RAF Regiment, I knew nothing about the POW 'Death Marches', until a mutual friend mentioned my name to Mrs Jessie Clews.

I am therefore indebted to Mrs Clews who approached me regarding compiling and publishing a story written by her late husband, Flt.Lt. Philip Henry Clews. Philip had hand-written his experience as a POW just before he died on the 19th February 2003 at the age of 82 years. This story has most certainly opened my eyes to the horrific experience he suffered, and to the thousands of others who suffered like him. Many of them paid with their lives, never to be seen by their loved ones ever again. May they not have died in vain!

It was an awful experience being a Prisoner of War in Europe during World War II, but there was no shame, each one can be proud and hold their head high, I for one salute them!

Not like the Japanese who felt it was a disgrace to be captured and interned, not only for themselves, but also for their families, hence the reason many gave false names. Harry Gordon highlights this in his book, **DIE LIKE THE CARP**! This is the story of the greatest POW escape ever, that was first published in 1978 and tells in detail what became one of the best-kept secrets of World War II.

The camp was at Cowra in NSW, Australia, and the incident took place in the early hours of the 5th August 1944 when over a thousand Japanese prisoners made a mass escape. Four Australian soldiers were killed and two hundred and forty-seven Japanese, the remainder were captured within nine days.

It was January 1984 when I paid a visit to the site that is just rubble and long grass. However, the cemetery that is close by is the only Japanese cemetery in Australia, and in an adjoining cemetery the Australian soldiers are buried, and both cemeteries are immaculate.

What I didn't bargain on finding in the cemetery where the Australians are buried, was the grave of a British Airman. This number might have a figure missing, 102957 Cpl. R.C. Carter, RAF, died 2nd December 1945 aged 24 years. I have never found the answer why he died in Australia?

Referring to the bog mentioned in the story by Philip Clews, I have vast experience of bogs going back to the 1920's and 30's. We lived in the country where the bog was a single bench type seat over a vault that had to be emptied every year. It was housed in a small wooden shed down the garden path, a very draughty, cold and dismal place that had to be visited every day, even in the depth of winter. I suppose one good thing about those visits, apart from the obvious, was catching up on all the news, newspapers being in abundance because there was no such thing as toilet rolls.

Then towards the end of 1944 and the early part of 1945, 2831 RAF Regiment Squadron was housed in a small camp in the village of Sancourt between Cambrai and Douai in Northern France. We had a communal bog with perhaps fourteen/sixteen holes in a long wooden bench over a trench. The thing I remember most about that abode, was the strong smell of lime that was used in the trench, for whatever reason, it really penetrated the nostrils. But we did not suffer the traumatic experience of severe dysentery and a queue waiting for the next vacant place, that must have been so degrading and humiliating.

Flt.Lt. Clews was only a Pilot Officer when he operated as a Navigator on a four-engine Handley Page Halifax Bomber. No doubt many such stories could be told, but this is Philip's story how the crew endured twenty-nine hazardous bombing raids over enemy territory. But their good luck ran out when a German night fighter shot down their aircraft on the thirtieth mission, just a few minutes after successfully delivering a load of bombs over Magdeburg in Germany. Mrs Clews informs me that her husband said the mission was fated from the start. The remark by one of the Gunners just before they boarded the plane saying "I hope we don't come home tonight", all because he had got a girl in trouble, was not a good start to a bombing mission.

Then of course, a night fighter attacked them as they prepared to return to base and their aircraft was shot down, the result being they had to 'hit the silk', as they say. Subsequently P/O Clews became a member of the famous 'Caterpillar Club'. Membership being open to: **'Anyone who saves his life by baling out of a stricken aircraft and lands safely, using a parachute of Irvin design regardless of manufacture'.**

P/O Clews fall was cushioned when he landed in snow covered

enemy territory. What followed for Philip were some horrendous days of walking and hiding, then eventually capture by the Germans. Philip found that walking in snow wearing flying boots was cumbersome and not very good for the feet, it produced awful blisters that still required attention when returning home on leave for six weeks after his return to the UK.

Philip Clews was one of thousands of POWs held in prison camps across Germany, there fear was being killed by the Germans as they retreated in the face of advancing Russian and American troops. But in the depth of winter and without adequate clothing and food, they were forced to march hundreds of miles away from the advancing troops who may have liberated them. Many died of disease, starvation, exhaustion, and those who survived suffered for many years after they were released, as did Philip Clews.

It is difficult to comprehend the suffering endured by all the POWs. Philip Clews for example, lost a lot of weight and was looking extremely gaunt when he arrived home on six weeks leave. He needed a lot of loving care by his wife to get him back on the road to some normality and better health.

The story involves one of the magnificent aircraft of World War II, the Handley Page Halifax Bomber that made a huge contribution to the war effort from 1941 to 1945, even though the famous Lancaster over shadowed it. It is interesting to note that during my tour of duty stationed at RAF Tangmere in 1942/43, several times around 25 or 30 four-engine bombers arrived at the station in the early hours of the morning that I helped to refuel. Having been on a long haul bombing raid they didn't have enough fuel to get back to their own station in Lincolnshire or South Yorkshire, or so we were informed. The majority of the aircraft were Lancaster's, but there were one or two Stirlings, which was another fine aircraft, and there was always a few Halifaxes, see my report on the Handley Page Halifax later in the book

Having kept my feet firmly on the ground – well not quite being a driver in the RAF Regiment, I have had problems with Flt. Lt. Clews navigator's terms which he didn't explain. For example 'G' or 'Gee', which I have been informed is a navigational aid, and 'DR' is Direct Reckoning, the latter of course in transport terms was Dispatch Rider. I have found nothing that indicates P/O Clews operated the H2S radar equipment, although Group Captain Hollis of 578 Squadron Burn Association informs me it is quite possible this bombing aid could have been fitted to Philip's aircraft.

I hope therefore that my interpretations are correct based on information received from various quarters. Should this not be so, then I stand to be corrected and will appreciate the correct information.

I also hope the interpretation of the abbreviations later in the book helps those readers who are not familiar with RAF jargon. The 'double talk' we had in a small close knit group of drivers and HQ staff in 2748 Squadron RAF Regiment in 1941 to 1944 often took some comprehending. For example one of our group lived only a short train ride from one particular camp and was therefore able to get home more often than those of us who lived further a-field. He always said he had to keep going home to see how his 'spuds' *(Lincolnshire expression of potatoes or 'tates')* were progressing. Then it was realised he didn't have a garden big enough to grow them, and it was not in the growing season anyway, but he did have a very loving wife!

A word about the poems that have been included, I'm sure you will agree they are relevant to the story and are nostalgic to say the least. My poetic friend, Victor Cavendish, wrote 'Stand Those Three Towers' that refers to Lincoln Cathedral, and Philip Clews refers to the Cathedral in his story. Although some of the poems were written in favour of the Lancaster, they can be attributed to the Halifax.

Victor Cavendish is ex-RAF as also was the late John Walsh. Both poets had the knack of looking back in time when those poems were written and relived nostalgic memories, also expressing the feelings and sentiments of all RAF ranks whether aircrew or grounds staff. Both of those groups integrated during World War II to form a formidable force that outwitted our enemies in the air.

Stanley Naylor. January 2004.

HOME RUN

Begone the night for we bring her home,
    Far below us the cold North Sea,
Now Dawn stands high in the paling sky
    And we fly with our spirits free.

Revive new hope now we live again,
    Gone the fear that haunts our flight,
Fades the threat of death as we guide her West
    And our faithful Lanc rides light.

We shall not dwell on our trip to hell,
    Far behind us the hostile sky,
Seven still fly strong to the Merlin's song
    And the miles to home run by.

        © *John R. Walsh February 1986.*

Courage by Robert Browning,

One who never turned his back but marched breast forward,
Never doubted clouds would break,
Never dreamed, though right were worsted, wrong would triumph,
Held we fall to rise, are baffled to fight better,
Sleep to wake.

STAND THOSE THREE TOWERS.

Stand those three towers still a-pointing
    In the dawn light, stark and clear?
Does the ghostly roar of the 'Lanc' still soar
    O'er the fields of Lincolnshire?

Do the shades of Ancient Briton;
    Of Roman, Saxon, Dane;
Still stand and gaze with mute amaze
    On the ghosts who throng the plain?

Ghosts of the flower of England;
    Of Empire and allied kin;
Are they still in sight in the darkening light?
    Each dusk as the night rolls in?

Ghosts of Geordie, Scouse and Cockney,
    Of Yellowbelly and Tyke;
Do they fly again over Martin Fen;
    O'er Grimsby and Boston Dyke?

And of Paddy, Jock and Taffy;
    Of Aussie, Canuck and Yank.
Are they flying still over Lindum Hill,
    O'er the Wash and the Humber Bank?

And the Freedom Men of Europe;
    New Zealand and Afric' dark;
Do they still fly strong to the Merlin's song?
    And the sound of the Browning's bark?

Do those hosts of glad young warriors
    Still soar and fly and toil
And fight and die in an alien sky;
    Still rest in an alien soil?

Ah! Many the distant lonely cross
　And many the shattered 'plane,
Whose last home sight on a bombers' night
　Was a view of a Lincoln Lane.

Does that lumbering bus still rumble?
　Those lanes from – Thorpe to – by?
Does it still stop hard by the old churchyard?
　Where more of our brothers lie?

Sons of all the warring nations;
　The plain men and the brave.
All troubles past; they've found their last
　Safe home in an English grave.

While we, who they left behind them;
　We few, as our years grow old
Still fight and fly in their battle sky
　In dreams when the night is cold.

Ah! Lincoln! Our shire of memories
　From the dawn to the setting sun;
Your heath and fen will live again
　With us till our journey's run.

　　　　　© *Victor Cavendish.*

The Royal Air Forces Association Dedication.

In friendship and in service one to another, we are pledged to keep alive the memory of those of all Nations who died in the Royal Air Force and in the Air Forces of the Commonwealth. In their name we give ourselves to this noble cause. Proudly and thankfully, we will remember them.

Prisoner of War
My Horrendous March 1945.
by
Flt. Lt. Phillip Henry Clews ex-RAF.

My entry into this troubled world was on Tuesday 2nd August 1921 and I joined the Royal Air Force (RAF) in February 1942 at the age of 20 years. I was issued with RAF No. 1582779 and the rank of AC2. The first six weeks involved basic training that included inoculations, vaccination, issue of kit, square bashing, PT, how to use a rifle and much more that every erk had to learn and so get initiated into the RAF.way of life. I later attained the rank of AC1 and then graduated to LAC on the 29th October 1942.

The first fourteen months of my service career was not very exciting, then from the 5th April to the 1st October 1943 I was on various courses at No. 1 Central Navigation School, Rivers, Manitoba in Canada. This involved navigation – practical and theory, meteorology, map reading, signals, photography and armament. During the time at Manitoba I completed 82 hours 20 minutes daytime flying and 37 hours at night. Suffice is to say that I qualified as a fully-fledged Navigator and was awarded my Air Navigation Badge on the 1st October 1943 with the rank of Sergeant. Then lo and behold I was promoted to Pilot Officer number 184919 on the 19th September 1944.

There were further navigation courses on returning to the UK that included parachute and dinghy drill that added another 24 hours 50 minutes daytime and 18 hours and 5 minutes at night to my total flying time. A posting followed this to 21 O.T.U. (Operation Training Unit) RAF Moreton-in-Marsh.

RAF Station, Moreton-in-Marsh was an Operational Training Station in 91 Bomber Group. The Station was situated some 15/16 miles south of Stratford-on-Avon in Gloucestershire, bordered by the A429 and A44 highways. The Station opened in 1941 and closed in 1955, total personnel 2,523 including 436 WAAF.

Pilots, Navigators, Wireless operators, Bomb Aimers and Gunners assembled at this training station. Hence a six-man crew was formed consisting of:-

Pilot –	F/O (Bob) Robert Lenard Maloney; RAAF, AUS417657
Bomb Aimer –	Sgt (Taffy) Williams; RAF.
Wireless Operator –	Flt/Sgt (Tom) Charles Thomas Moore, RAAF AUS429471.
Navigator -	P/O (Phil) Philip Henry Clews. RAF No. 184918.
Gunner -	Sgt. Howard Gordon Skeats, RAF No 1432264.
Gunner -	Sgt. (Bill) Thomas William Spencer, RAF No 1436676.

Now that a crew was established, we had to be trained to operate as a fighting unit. Bob had been used to flying solo and did not find it easy in taking instructions from a navigator on the first two training flights. At first he completely ignored me, he really had a will of his own. Then we got lost on one of the training sessions, (Pilot wiser than Navigator!), but he eventually realised he had to take note of my instructions.

Having completed 54 hours 45 minutes daytime flying and 43 hours 55 minutes at night at 21 OTU as a full compliment of six in a twin engine Vickers Wellington Bomber, we were considered to be a competent crew. Total flying time to date 161 hours 55 minutes daytime and 99 hours at night.

We were informed that we were to be transferred to another flight to fly a new aircraft to the Middle East, fortunately this was cancelled. Instead we were posted to 1658 H.C.U. RAF Station at Riccall in Yorkshire, No 7 Bomber Command. The station was located ten miles south of York, but north of Selby beside the A19, it opened in 1942 and closed in 1946. Total personnel 1,787 including 341 WAAF.

1658 H.C.U. was a Heavy Conversion Unit where we moved from two engine aircraft to four engine aircraft. Therefore on arrival we encountered our first four engine Handley Page Halifax, and we acquired our seventh member of the crew, Sgt. Cyril George Atkins a Flight Engineer. No. 1594303.

After an initial trip for the pilot to get accustomed to flying a four engine aircraft, we were allocated an aircraft to practise my skills crawling around England with the aid of the GEE navigation system.

It was an adventure on which I took the crew wherever they wanted to go! We hedge hopped Blackpool Pier, we shot up the Grand at Leeds, and also my home in a small village in Lincolnshire. It was great fun, but on the serious side it sharpened up my use of the dials on the GEE instrument. It also demonstrated the crew had faith in my ability to navigate a true course.

The GEE box was a navigational device that was a useful piece of equipment that enabled me on a number of occasions to accurately get a "fix" on our position, either in finding the target or on returning to base. The device received signals from stations in England up to a distance of some 400 miles. The reception of a good signal depended on our height because of the curvature of the earth, the best results at that distance was around 20,000 feet, but it could vary. Unfortunately the Germans developed a jamming system that was effective over their country.

Flying time on the Halifax four engine aircraft at 1658 H.C.U., RAF Riccall was 22 hours 20 minutes daytime and 7 hours at night.

Total flying time to date 184 hours 15 minutes daytime and 106 hours at night. But our fun days were over, the day had arrived when we were informed we were being posted to an operational unit.

It was the 28th July 1944 when we were transferred to RAF Burn in No. 4 Bomber Command Group. The station was situated beside the A19 highway south of Selby in Yorkshire, it opened in 1942 and closed in 1946, it had a compliment of 2,081 personnel including 276 WAAF. 578 Squadron was formed in January 1944 at RAF Snaith and moved to Burn in February 1944. It was therefore a well-established operational Squadron by the time we joined them at the end of July.

It was owing to the loss of four aircraft in a raid that we were rushed in as a replacement to join 'C' Flight. Bob, our pilot was the only one of our crew to get any familiarisation practise by having a trip with another crew on a bombing mission that gave him some experience of what was to come within the next few days, weeks and months.

We were eventually called to the briefing room that was heavily guarded against intruders. When the crews were all present, the cover was removed from the map on the wall and we were informed of the location of our target.

After all our intensive training, this was the crunch, could we uphold the honour of Bomber Command and complete our mission? It was therefore with much apprehension that we boarded Halifax LK-V and departed on our first bombing mission on time on the 5th August 1944. Our target, the Flying Bomb sites at Le Foret de Nieppe, this was termed a 'Lillyput' incident, meaning a tiny or small operation that we successfully completed in daylight in 3 hours 20 minutes.

We completed two more short daytime missions and one at night, and then we were briefed for our first long-haul mission to be undertaken at night to Russelsheim near Frankfurt in Germany. This was going to be a much tougher mission, we were informed that navigation aids could be jammed by a sea of "grass" through which no signals could be read. The flight plan was duly completed, the route to follow being equated by the met forecasts.

The outward journey was uneventful, apart from being apprehensive travelling so deep into enemy territory. The bombs were dropped successfully and we set course on the long leg to the French Coast using proven mist winds. We had been travelling about an hour when one of the Gunners asked "Where are we Navigator?". To which I replied "I don't know but I'm not lost". This was true because I had absolute faith in my calculations. We duly arrived on time over the French Coast and arrived back to base after being airborne for 6 hours and 10 minutes.

We continued bombing targets as designated by 'Bomber' Harris, this included daylight raids on the 'Flying Bomb' launch pads that reduced the sites considerably of the dreaded German menace. There were also the raids to industrial sites and marshalling yards including, Caen, Hazelbrook, Somain, Triemont, Keil, Sterkrade, Brest, Hamburg, Munster, Wilhelmshaven, St. Etienne, Essen and Duisberg. None of them healthy places to visit on a bombing mission, the enemy had a nasty habit of trying to shoot us down, either by guns from below or a night fighter getting on our tail on the outward or return journey. The latter finally happened on a raid later on.

Some of the raids were trouble free, but it still played havoc with the nerves. We were not so lucky on the 16th August 1944 with LK-V on the Kiel Canal bombing mission carrying 1 x 2,000 lb bomb and 13 x 90 - 4 lb incendiaries. We left our Yorkshire base and were on the direct route to the target in the early hours of the morning. On approaching the target, Tom, our wireless operator, informed us in his best Aussie voice that his radio equipment had packed-up. He also informed us that his book of rules stated "If your radio equipment packed up you should return to base". After a discussion amongst the whole crew, we made the decision to return home, it was then 'over to you Navigator'! This presented me with a problem, because most of our route had been spent travelling over the sea which had lacked the time to prove the met forecasts, so I was literally on my own. There being no aid to give me a clue where to go, and no DR (*Direct Reckoning)* ahead to give me time to find a position, I seized upon the best wind I could find. Bob, the pilot, was given height, course and speed to fly, and an E.T.A. (*Estimated Time of Arrival)* back at base. So we flew literally on a wing and a prayer up to the E.T.A. At that point we still were not sure where we were and was on the point of deciding to do a change on the E.T.A., when airfield lights proved we were over our own 'drome. We really had been travelling on a wing and a prayer, but I was very relieved my navigation had proved to be spot on! The trip had taken 5 hours and 55 minutes during the night.

There were many notable trips with the adrenaline running high and nerves shattered. None of them could be said to be routine, there was always apprehension, but at least the reception committee was not always active! Even so, we were aware the 'Reaper' was for ever present over enemy territory.

On the 16th November 1944 we were called upon to bomb the small town of Julich. This was carpet-bombing in daylight and the number of aircraft taking part in bombing Julich was 508, of which 413 were Halifaxes. There were three German towns bombed that day to assist the advancing American Army, so we were informed. Number of aircraft involved in the whole operation was 1,188, another awesome mission with so many aircraft taking part.

It was a clear day and we did our bombing run at 8,000 feet, but the Bomb Aimer missed his dropping point, so the skipper decided to try a second run. This was not such a good idea, we circled the target and came in again and consequently we were now at the rear of all the aircraft and an easy target. Then suddenly German 88 dual purpose guns opened fire that was far to close for comfort, so we got out quickly after delivering our load of bombs without too much damage to the aircraft. Entry in my logbook states 'Accurate Flack – Orbit once'. This trip took 4 hours and 45 minutes,

Christmas Eve 1944 was a day to remember. We were on stand by and were called to the briefing room early in the day. There was a lot of fog about nation-wide and so we could not believe that we were to be sent out on a mission in such appalling weather, and on Christmas Eve. But there was a daylight raid planned on the Mulheim Essen airfield, and the route was slap over territory where the natives were not very friendly. The tragedy was that the 'gaggle' that was to form the main force never happened. We were in the first Squadrons to take off, but owing to the fog the 2nd and 3rd waves never left the ground. We proceeded on our way, still looking for the rest of the units that should have been in the middle of the 'gaggle', but were of course, none existent. This meant we had to go through the dropping zone like sitting ducks, but we reached it safely and were successful in dropping our bombs on the target. Although we had received a 'warm welcome', fortunately not a single plane was lost. So we flew back home leaving a badly scarred airfield, although shell shocked, we were thankfully still in one piece.

The journey home was uneventful except for the fog that shrouded the country. It was still daylight as we headed for home, our route taking us over Lincoln where we saw a most incredible sight. There was the beautiful Cathedral with its magnificent towers sticking out above the fog. I shall never forget the thrill that unique picture gave all the crew, it is certainly imprinted in my mind.

We travelled on to Burn and found no visible signs of the Station, in fact the fog was so thick it made it impossible for us to make a safe landing. Unfortunately Burn was not equipped with FIDO, (*Fog Investigation Dispersal Operation*) that had been installed on a few airfields. This was a pipe system that ran the full length on each side of the runway with outlet valves at regular intervals. Engines, usually Perkins Diesel, pumped the low-grade fuel down the pipes forcing it through the valves spraying it some thirty feet high. When the fuel was ignited it created enormous amount of heat that would lift a fog 700 to 800 feet high and was really spectacular, but it allowed aircraft to land safely.

Because of the thick fog at Burn, we were subsequently diverted to RAF Waltham just south of Grimsby beside the A16 on the Lincolnshire coast. I believe the Station was officially known as RAF Grimsby because that was the nearest town, but Waltham was the nearest village and railway station, barely three miles away. The airfield however, was on the edge of the hamlet of Holton-le-Clay, it opened in 1941 and closed in 1946. Total personnel 1,682 including 286 WAAF.

The fog was clear when we arrival at Waltham and we were placed in a queue of aircraft waiting to land, this meant we were stacked up over the Station to wait our turn.

This situation did not please Bob our pilot, because he was worried about our airworthiness, the starboard outer engine was dodgy, it had been vibrating badly and was getting worse. Bob was not very happy about the state of the aircraft at all and called up flying control with a very descriptive expletive that we needed to land, and then the engine dropped! (*Meaning it was u/s – unserviceable*). We were finally given permission to land that was completed safely, but Bob got a ticking off for using bad language in front of the females in flying control, even though they may have heard it all before. The trip had taken 5 hours in daylight.

This was Christmas Eve 1944 and what a way to spend it in our respective messes away from our home base with DIY entertainment. We were given plenty of food, but had to kip down (*sleep*) in chairs in the officer's mess, all the time protesting that we wanted to go home, home being RAF Burn.

Christmas morning dawned and we prepared to go back to Burn by bus, but the Waltham transport would go no further than half way. It was therefore decided the transport from the two stations would meet at Brigg and, for whatever reason, the Police were informed of the invasion of a crowd of airman wanting to celebrate Christmas. On arrival at Brigg we had a few drinks and then spilled out in the street. Imagine what was happening in the town with the unusual sight of all the crew in flying kit. But we were well received, despite the locals having their festivities upset by a gang of unruly airmen, well it was Christmas! They even produced a Christmas cake and the party spirit was warming up when our bus arrived to enable us to continue our journey back to Burn. On arriving back at camp, despite the fact it was time for Christmas dinner, we invaded the mess demanding our usual meal of eggs, bacon and chips that we normally received after returning from an operation. But the kitchen was all geared up ready to serve the traditional dinner on this festive day, including the turkey and Christmas pudding. We had no option therefore but to go to the billet and get dressed up – best blue - and return to the mess where we enjoyed an excellent meal of Christmas fare.

No doubt I am biased as regards the Halifax Bomber, but it was almost as famous as the Lancaster, it was certainly a more versatile aircraft performing many rolls. But to prove my point on its bombing roll, here are the figures of Halifax aircraft used on raids over enemy territory in which I was involved.

'T a/c' in brackets denotes total number of all makes of aircraft involved on that particular mission, the number of Halifax aircraft involved on each raid is highlighted.

August 1944, 11 missions completed.
Flying Bomb Sites, day 3 hours. (T a/c 742)
469 Halifaxes.
Hazelbrouck, day 3 hours 10 minutes. (T a/c 62)
51 Halifaxes.
Caen area, (Army co-op) night 4 hrs 20 mins. (T a/c 1,000)
392 Halifaxes
Marshalling Yards, Somain, day 4 h. 15 mins. (T a/c 469)
169 Halifaxes.
Russelheim carrying 1 x 2,000 lb bomb and 13 x 90--4 lb incendiaries, night 6 hours 10 minutes. (T a/c 297)
96 Halifaxes.
Nine airfields were attacked, ours was Triemont, day 4 hrs.
1,000 + aircraft involved in the whole operation,
385 Halifaxes.
Kiel – same bomb load as above, night 5 hours 55 minutes.
(T a/c 348)
144 Halifaxes.
Sterkrade Ruhr Valley, night 4 hours 45 minutes. (T a/c 234)
210 Halifaxes.
Brest, night 5 hours 35 minutes. (T a/c 334)
284 Halifaxes.
Honberg – The Ruhr, day 4 hours 30 minutes. (T a/c 243)
216 Halifaxes.

Pas de Calais, Flying-Bomb Sites, day 3 hours 40 minutes.
(T a/c 150)
77 Halifaxes.

September 1944, five missions completed.
Munster, day 4 hours 20 minutes. (T a/c 124)
119 Halifaxes.
Wilhelmshaven, day 3 hours 15 minutes. (T a/c 184)
133 Halifaxes.
Kiel, night 3 hours 20 minutes. *(Aborted?)* (T a/c 490)
173 Halifaxes.
St Etienne, day 3 hours 15 minutes.
Number of aircraft not recorded.
Bottrop, day 4 hours 35 minutes. (T a/c 136)
101 Halifaxes.

October 1944, four missions completed.
Essen, night 5 hours 10 minutes. (T a/c 1,055)
463 Halifaxes.
This was the second biggest bombing mission that I had ever been involved, they were awesome.
Walcheren, day 3 hours 40 minutes. (T a/c 277)
155 Halifaxes.
Walcheren, day 3 hours 10 minutes. (T a/c 358)
128 Halifaxes.
Cologne, night 5 hours. (T a/c 905)
438 Halifaxes.

November 1944. Four missions completed.
Julich, day 4 hours 45 minutes. (T a/c 508)
413 Halifaxes.
Munster, day 5 hours 20 minutes. (T a/c 479)
367 Halifaxes.
Sterkrade, night 5 hours 45 minutes. (T a/c 270)
232 Halifaxes.
Essen, night 5 hours 40 minutes. (T a/c 316)
270 Halifaxes.

December 1944. Three missions completed.
Essen, night 5 hours 35 minutes. (T a/c 540)
163 Halifaxes.
Duisburg, night 6 hours 50 minutes. (T a/c 523)
418 Halifaxes.
Mulheim & Essen, day 5 hours. (T a/c 338)
248 Halifaxes.

January 1945. Two missions completed.
Mannheim, night 6 hours 30 minutes.
Number of aircraft used on this mission is not known.
Hanau/Frankfurt, night 6 hours 25 minutes. (T a/c 482)
314 Halifaxes.

By this time we had completed twenty-nine operations and had been given a well deserved leave. Then on the 16th January 1945 we were briefed for our thirtieth *(30th)* operation. This would have been our last operation of our first tour and we would have had a long rest before embarking on a second tour. Our target was Magdeburg that involved 371 aircraft including **320 Halifaxes.**

Our eight-man crew was:

F/O Robert Leonard Maloney, RAAF, AUS417657 - Pilot.	Died.
F/O Ivor Glyn Owen, RAF, 146350 Bomb Aimer.	Died.
P/O Philip Henry. Clews, RAF, 184918 Navigator.	POW.
P/O Patrick James Fitzgerald, RCAF, J89601 Air Gunner.	POW.
F/S Charles Thomas Moore, RAAF, AUS429471 WOP/AG.	POW.
Sgt Cyril George Atkins, RAF, 1594303 Flight Engineer.	POW.
Sgt Howard Gordon Skeats, RAF, 1432264 Air Gunner.	POW.
Sgt Thomas William Spencer, RAF, 1436676 Rear Gunner.	POW.

As you can see it was a mixed Commonwealth crew, one Canadian, two Australians and five British.

After briefing we were transported to the dispersal point where our kite, *(Aircraft)* Halifax III NA603 LK-T was ready for the mission, having been prepared by a dedicated ground crew. We were standing by the aircraft smoking and relating what we had been doing during the recent leave. Perhaps we were a little apprehensive, but savouring the short time we had just enjoyed with our loving families. Now the chat was very ordinary until Gordon, the mid-upper Gunner arrived. He had some very surprising news, he had got a girl in Leeds "in trouble", which probably was not the first as both Sgt. Gunners were very promiscuous. He then came out with the words "I hope we don't come home tonight". There was deathly silence amongst the rest of the crew. With those words ringing in my ears I felt the mission was jinxed from the start.

We boarded the aircraft and moved to our take off position. After leaving the tarmac and the wheels were up, we set course for the target and crossed the North Sea without incident. At a designated position we altered course due South over land. After a further navigational alteration on our course we approached Magdeburg from the North and made a successful bombing run over the target. The Flight Engineer checked that all the bombs had been dropped and I gave the Pilot height and course to travel home.

No sooner had we reached the right height and set on the new course for home, when all hell broke loose, a German night fighter was attacking us, possibly an ME110. Suddenly from anticipating a nice quite ride home, we were in serious trouble, because the two starboard engines were ablaze. We attached our parachutes for immediate use, but were reluctant to leave the aircraft. Then the Skipper informed us he could not hold the aircraft for much longer and said "Well fellers I guess you had better hit the silk".

My escape was to stand up from my navigation table to reveal a hatch, which I pulled up and jumped through the opening. It was quite an eerie feeling, I was falling fast doing great somersaults, and suddenly realised it was time I pulled the ripcord, this released a billow of silk that slowed down my descent. Although I thought I was dropping slowly, I was still falling fairly fast, but fortunately a blanket of snow broke my fall. I quickly removed my parachute and buried it in the snow.

I had seen the plane go down and wondered what had happened to the Skipper and the rest of my fellow crew members. I later found out that an entry in my log book referring to Halifax LK-T reads as follows:

"**Attacked by Night Fighter from below and ahead. Starboard inner engine set on fire and petrol tank holed. Bomb Aimer killed. Orders to bale out at 15,000 feet. The Skipper went down with A/C and was killed. Remainder of crew POW**".

Our aircraft was shot down some 650 yards south of Gross

Vahlberg and just three miles WSW of Schoppenstedt. F/O Owen was killed when we were hit by the night fighter and was originally buried at Vahlberg Grossunderklein, but was finally buried in Hanover British Military War Cemetery. F/O Maloney was originally buried in the Margraten Cemetery, his final resting place is in the Venray War Cemetery.

But here I was having suddenly jumped from being cocooned in an aircraft with a dedicated crew, to being alone in Germany that was still a hostile country, and I had no idea where the rest of the crew had landed. Although I realised I was some miles from the Dutch border, I was committed to try and get home. I set off walking due west until I found a haystack about five feet high that I dived into to rest and collect my thoughts.

I pondered about being taken prisoner, but my main object remained, I had to try and get back to the UK, but it was a daunting task dressed in a rather conspicuous RAF flying suit. I decided to rest during the day and try travelling at night, so I stayed under cover for the remainder of the daylight hours listening to the sounds of farm animals.

Immediately it was dark, I moved from the stack leaving the sounds of the farm animals behind. I continued to go due west, trying to keep the Pole Star on my right shoulder, hoping that I would eventually reach either the Dutch or Belgian border. I soon realised that walking in flying boots was not an ideal way of travelling over snow covered ground. But I pressed on travelling over many fields until arriving at a small river. Which way should I go? Having decided to follow the river to the right for some distance and finding no means of crossing, I returned to the starting point and proceeded to follow the river to the left. Lo and behold a short distance from where I had first encountered the river there was a bridge, I crossed quickly and continued over more frozen fields, still finding it difficult walking in those flying boots. There was another problem when I encountered obstacles across my path causing me to keep changing direction.

Eventually I came to the edge of a forest where entry was not easy and progress was difficult in the thick undergrowth amongst the trees. Then I heard howling that sounded like wolves, not waiting to confirm my suspicions, I left the forest quicker than I had entered.

I was cold, wet and very hungry, the only thing keeping me going were the small balls of snow that I kept sucking, but this made my tongue very sore. On the edge of the forest I found a heap of potato haulms that I tried to use as a blanket and snatch some sleep until daylight. This was not very successful, sleeping being almost none existent, and my face was now a mess with a beard covered in muck, I must have looked a terrible sight.

I changed my plan from resting during the day and started to cross the forest in daylight, hoping to get through to the other side before dark. This plan was soon shattered when I came across a band of woodchoppers. Changing direction, I managed to go round them without being seen, then sat down to consider my position once again. Having decided to press on, I proceeded through the forest, then after another change in direction I emerged out of the forest and continued walking along a track on the perimeter of this dense wood. Eventually I came upon hay covering what turned out to be a heap of turnips. I dived under the hay to try and get a warm place to have a sleep. This was not to be, because I heard a noise outside and then the spikes of a hand fork appeared taking out turnips. It was a hard and difficult time dodging those spikes, but eventually the intruder got enough turnips, covered up the heap and departed, leaving behind a very scared, sweaty, undiscovered airman.

I stayed with the turnips for the rest of the day until I noticed far down the track there was a cottage. By this time I had been without food and drink for several days so I was desperate, my body could no longer stay without water, and I needed some solid food and warmth. Making my way to the cottage I knocked on the door but no one answered. I knocked a second time, this time the door opened slowly and a little old lady took one look at my dishevelled appearance and immediately shut the door. This was a calamity, I know I really looked a mess and because my spirit was at a low ebb, and much to my dismay, I actually sat down and cried. But I decided I was not beaten yet and knocked a third time. This time the door was opened by an old gentleman who jabbered away in German, which meant we couldn't understand each other. By some stroke of luck we managed to stumble through in French, this gave us a limited means of communication. However, I was eventually taken to a house at the rear of the cottage by the farmer where he kept me, he was accompanied by a woman believed to be his wife.

It was at this point that I asked for a drink of water that was immediately given to me and it couldn't have tasted better, it really was life saving. But I wasn't so lucky when I asked for food, I didn't get any, perhaps the communication was not so good after all. The farmer was a little fat man, who had already called for a guard, but then he started to rant and rave pointing to a large picture on the wall of Hitler, and the woman was pointing to a photograph on the dresser. This appeared to upset her and caused her to cry, but I could make no connection. Then a couple entered the room that I learned was a daughter and son-in-law. This had a considerable effect on the old man because it certainly quietened his berating of me.

I have since found out that during the last year of the war, German civilians were encouraged by their hierarchy to inflict their vengeance indiscriminately on any captured allied airman for the damage they had done to Germany on their bombing missions. This may be the reason for the behaviour of my civilian captors, because it was very disturbing and demoralising to say the least.

The guard who collected me was a Corporal who was always in a hurry and I found it difficult keeping up with him. I was taken to what appeared to be the front room of a house that was occupied by two old men and two boys. One of the men had been a prisoner in the First World War and said he had been well looked after by the British, so while I was a prisoner in that house he would look after me. He helped me to have a wash that was refreshing and then made some toast. The two boys produced their aircraft book and we had quiet a laugh about planes. I was made cosy in a nice warm room and for the first time since leaving the doomed aircraft, I fell into a sound sleep.

In the morning a car arrived with a driver and the Corporal guard. I was escorted from the village to a Luftwaffe fighter station where I saw enemy planes complete with Swastikas. I was not there to admire the aircraft of course, but to be placed in a dirty single cell with a dirty blanket. Well I thought I was alone in what was supposed to be a single cell until I started scratching, it was then I realised the place was lousy with fleas, and they sure could bite. After a miserable night I was pleased to leave my flea ridden cell and it took me a long time to get rid of the little devils.

The same Corporal collected me and he made his way to a railway station and so to the ticket office. We boarded a windowless train and travelled to another station, the name is not remembered. The Corporal dashed off leaving his prisoner hardly able to keep up with him, his target was the service canteen where I managed to get a little refreshment of some description.

We left the canteen and found the platform full of German personnel, or perhaps some were refugees, but my Corporal was still in a great hurry steering me through the throng. We boarded a train that was packed tight with people and so we had to travel in the luggage carriage, but managed to get a position near the doorway that enabled me to get a bit of fresh air, because the air inside was foul. We passed through various towns that had received the full might of the Allied Air Forces, in fact all the railway stations were a mess with trucks smashed and derailed with just a single line through the wreckage.

The Krauts (*Germans*) in the carriage kept eyeing me up, because I was still very conspicuous travelling in my full RAF flying gear, but the moment of tension passed and we settled down to travel on to Frankfurt. On reaching the station, the Corporal rushed off to the equivalent of our NAFFI and managed to get us some more refreshments of sorts.

After leaving the canteen we boarded the train and travelled in a very uncomfortable windowless carriage. It was very cold and I thought I would freeze to death, but it was only a short distance to a junction where we departed from the train.

The ground was covered in deep snow and I was still having trouble walking in flying boots. I fought on gallantly trying to keep up with my guard, but was getting further behind. Then into sight came a German Officer who stopped the Corporal, he apparently was asking why he was letting his prisoner drag along so far behind. Even though I could not speak the German language, it was obvious the Corporal got a severe reprimand. This resulted in the Corporal slowing down to my pace that was very slow.

We eventually reached the infamous interrogation camp of Dulag Luft that is located near Frankfurt am Main where most captured airmen were first interned. I was stripped of all my clothes, the Germans were searching for anything that might be of interest to them. When the clothes were returned, they were minus the £5 note that had been secreted in the fur lining of one of my flying boots.

I was placed in solitary confinement in a cell with a temperature that varied from hot to cold. The size of the cell was approximately 7/8 feet high, 6/7 feet wide and 10/12 feet long. Furniture was sparse, a table, chair and a bed, there was an electric bell to call the guard, but that did not mean he always responded, not that I used the bell very often anyway. All aircrew were confined in these single cells, and my first confined session lasted for twenty-four hours, during which time an arrival form was completed that included these questions as far as I can remember. Service number; Rank and name; Nationality; Trade; Date of Birth and where born; Air Force; Squadron; Station; Type of Aircraft; Members of Crew; Wounded; Killed; POW. My Religion; Married; Children; Home address; Next of Kin.

After this confined session I was taken to an interrogation room where I was asked many searching questions, including some of the above, by an interrogator who could speak very good English and so appeared to be a very pleasant person, or was he? My reply to all his questions was always the same - number, rank and name – 184918 PO Clews. Eventually I was returned to my cell where the minimum of food was brought to me at certain times of the day.

My second visit to the interrogation room was the following day when cigarettes were produced, this seemed to be a softening-up tactic that made me very cautious. Many more searching questions were asked of which I am sure he already knew the answers, because I was informed other members of the crew who had escaped from the doomed aircraft were also in captivity and are believed to have given standard answers to the questions. However, because I was a Commissioned Officer with information not privy to some members of the crew, I'm sure the questions put to me were far more searching, but my answers remained the same, number, rank and name.

The questioning went on for about two weeks, by this time I was allowed to have a shave and finally a ghastly rough shower, but never the less it was a blessing in any language. The interrogation ceased, perhaps because it was thought I was a waste of time, and I was then transferred to what was called by the internees, the propaganda block. This was a small block with a little more comfort where we were all permitted to mingle together. The Germans tried preaching propaganda to us with questions such as "Why are you fighting, if you defeat us you will only have to do battle with the Russians?" This propaganda war went on for several days, probably long enough for a large enough gaggle to be collected, then we were passed on to Vetzph what is best described as a holding unit or transit camp.

When a large enough gaggle of prisoners had been gathered, we were herded onto a battered train with sides boarded up, presumably to keep us in. The floors were badly damaged, the results of Allied bombing. We had an uncomfortable journey that lasted several days. Finally we arrived at Stalag 13A at Bad Sulzbach, Rosenburg, that was rather shoddy to say the least

Then a few weeks later we were joined by a number of prisoners believed to have come from Stalag 8C, Sagan, we were given to understand this was the camp where a number of prisoners had been shot, and those that arrived at our camp were the lucky ones.

With the new influx of prisoner's came a more amiable life, our meagre rations improved slightly, but food was not a priority for the Germans as far as prisoners were concerned. We were then operating the camp on military lines, if only to annoy the guards. Of course, we had to line up on the camp road each morning and night to be counted in hut order by the 'Goons', as we called the German guards. Heaven help us if any prisoner was missing, but there was often one in the bog who was probably suffering from diarrhoea, or the dreaded dysentery. This caused the guards to panic and was rather amusing in a bizarre sort of way, not amusing for the poor sod that daren't leave the latrine of course, he had his own serious problems to contend with.

Time however, passed slowly and we had to provide our own sports and entertainment. I acquired a small chess set that passed away many long hours. (*Incidentally, I still have the set at home*)

Later things began to hot up with allied bombing being intensified. Permission was then granted to dig slit trenches outside each hut. The Americans therefore were very busy digging their trenches, but the RAF contingent never moved a muscle. Later on during night raids we could hear the Americans shouting and moving outside their huts, but again the RAF personnel never moved an inch.

The bombing became furious both by day and night. The Yanks bombed the town in three daylight raids in a row. Our camp was on the flight path and so we could watch the bombs being released in batches, praying there was no undershoot. The RAF Lancaster's dropping the largest bombs, 4,000 pounders mainly at night. We had dropped some big bombs that caused havoc, but these certainly created a hell of an explosion and must have been frightening, because the blasts from those dropped near our camp rocked the huts.

Then there was a surprise, one of my mates, 'Chuck' Wilson, from earlier days in the UK arrived in camp. His plane was shot down in Holland and most of his crew had made their way safely back to 'Blighty'. But 'Chuck' had been badly injured and had a spell in hospital, when he was fit he was transferred to join us in the prison camp. He had arrived with nothing, but I willingly shared what little I had accumulated.

The intake from Sagan got larger and so we moved to bigger premises next door. This was not a good move, the previous tenants had been dirty 'Frogs', (*Frenchmen*) the place was lousy, and I mean lousy, we were bitten for days until we eventually managed to clear the place, but it was a struggle living in such lousy dirty conditions.

Life carried on in a humdrum way until one morning we woke up to about eighteen inches of snow, which distracted us for a time. A lot of our time was spent making 'Klim Burners' from the ex-powdered milk tins, with a smaller tin fitted inside the Klim tin. By an arrangement of holes around the top of the inner tin and slots in the bottom, we were able to feed slivers of wood into the inner can and when lit was almost as good as a gas ring. Then we were threatened by the 'Goons' that if we removed anymore timber from the washhouse we would be shot. But it made no difference, we just carried on because we had to keep our fires burning.

It then became the topic that the war was creeping closer to us, and as early as March 1944, Camp Commandants had received instructions that in the case of imminent invasion by the Russians, all POW's were to be moved further into Germany. Subsequently we were told to evacuate the camp, which was to be done in an orderly fashion. The instruction from our own SAO (*Senior American Officer*) was to cause as much chaos as possible, which we tried to do as we evacuated the huts. On the other hand, the 'Yanks' marched out as if they were going on parade. The Germans then had a problem, they found it difficult, in fact almost impossible to control a column of men with very few guards, but they were carrying machine guns and they are a powerful deterrent. We were causing a lot of chaos, as instructed, because we had no idea where we were going and if the guards knew they were not telling us. Rumours were therefore rife about our destination, one being that we were to be marched to the Bavarian Alps and none of us wanted to go there. The chaos was getting the guards very angry and they threatened to put us on a train. Now this was something none of us wanted to do either, we dreaded the prospect of being forced to board a train. This was because trains were not marked indicating there were POW's on board, and allied planes were known to attack trains whether they were on the move, or in marshalling yards.

So we protested and eventually were allowed to keep on walking providing we obeyed our masters, which we did for a time. But we were short of food, it was in fact almost to the point of starvation to say the least, we would often walk all day without eating a crumb of anything at all. We were sleeping in barns specified by the Germans, so four of us formed a gang. At the next barn two grabbed all the bedding we required, this was mainly straw, and the other two searched for food by raiding hen houses for eggs, or whatever was available, because we were always desperate for something to fill our bellies. I have to say that although German style Red Cross Units provided some food parcels, the German guards took some of them because they were also short of food. They did provide some sort of medical facilities, which were far from adequate.

I was still walking in flying boots that was causing me serious problems. Consequently I was called into one of the German style Red Cross units to have my feet treated, they were absolutely covered in blisters. The remedy was simple, get a pair of scissors and cut away all the loose skin, then they sent me on my way. This really was an excruciating way of marching on feet that was practically bare. The big problem, and my fear, was not being able to get my boots on and not being able to walk in order to keep with the main column, because it was known that stragglers were taken into woods and shot.

Then I joined a party who had taken over the front room in a house where we stayed for a few days, this gave me some measure of respite. In the room was a radio on which we were able to listen to the true news from the BBC, this was very heartening. Between us we had a quantity of soap that we had saved from the few Red Cross parcels we had received. Soap being scarce in Germany during that period of the war it was a passport to anything. As our main problem was short of food, we were therefore able to barter one bar of soap for one large round loaf of bread that was a real luxury, and we loved it.

But our luxury abode was short lived, we had to take to the open road and move on. We plodded on until we reached a clear stream running from the Alps. This was much too inviting, so we all stripped off and jumped into the water and immediately jumped out, it was freezing cold. We then ventured in more slowly and managed to have a good wash that removed some of the dust from our travels, this proved to be very refreshing. Shortly after that experience I was feeling hungry, rummaging in my bag I found a tin of Red Cross salmon, one of the few things I had managed to scrounge from the parcels, opening it I then ate the lot. I have never been able to face salmon since.

The march was an experience I don't wish to repeat. Although we had a wash of sorts in the stream we had encountered, I was still wearing the same clothes that were now filthy and it was difficult keeping lice at bay. Sanitation was merely a word, so toilet needs was about as primitive as can be imagined. I was still having trouble with huge blisters on my feet that made walking very difficult. Sleeping arrangements was not always in a barn, so sleeping in the open during one of the coldest winters ever known in Germany meant it was almost impossible to sleep. We only had one blanket each, so two of us would huddle together and share our two blankets to try and get a bit of warmth. It really was freezing cold and in the morning we stamped our feet and batted our hands to try and get some circulation in our body. As already mentioned, food was absolutely inadequate to sustain the strength required on such a march. The Red Cross parcels, although few and far between, did provide some food but it was a matter of scrounging whatever food we could lay our hands on. Often there was only a potato, or a slice of black bread that the guards provided, some POW's ate pig food and a handful of grain pinched from a farm could be chewed on the march. Water was also in short supply and often it was contaminated, but we were desperate for liquid to wet parched lips and a dry mouth. Snow was again eaten, but it hardly provided any substance, and still made my mouth and tongue sore.

However, like many of my comrades I lost weight and no doubt looked just as gaunt and haggard as my walking companions. The main thing is that we managed to survive the terrible ordeal of what became known as 'The Bread March', because often that was all we got during the day. The march has also been referred to as 'The Death March', because some stragglers were shot. The Americans referred to these marches, and there was more than the one I was on, as 'The Boot Leather Express'. The actual distance we walked is not known, but it has been estimated to be at least one hundred to one hundred and twenty miles. Distance of course, just became a blur as the days dragged on, and I kept no records, survival at that point was far more important.

We eventually arrived at Stalag VIIA at Moosburg, Germany. The column had stretched some distance, probably a mile or two, and so it took a long time from the first part of the column getting to Moosburg and the last man arriving safely. The camp was situated twenty-two miles Northeast of Munich and about half-a-mile North of Moosburg in Germany.

I soon found out that Moosburg was the worst camp in which I had been interned. It was a camp in two parts separated by double barbed wire. We were one side of the wire and on the other side were thousands of Russian prisoners, both male and female.

Apparently the camp had been built on a swamp, hence it was ankle deep in mud when it rained, and in hot weather we were informed it was the haunt of mosquitoes. Thankfully we missed that invasion because we were back in Blighty before the summer.

Our sleeping arrangements allocated to us were three tier wooden bunks joined together into blocks of twelve, the object was to cram at least double the two hundred each building was intended to hold. During my time at Stalag VIIA at Moosburg, it was estimated that over one hundred thousand POW's of all nationalities were crammed in a space only built for ten to twelve thousand personnel.

There was only one cold water tap in our dilapidated building, which seemed to be the norm that we had to use for all our daily needs. Hunger was endued every day, what food we got was slices of black bread, this was akin to a flat hard biscuit and not easy to break. I'm not sure what it was made of, but it tasted like sawdust. Then there was a boiled potato or turnip, the latter reminded me of my resting-place in the heap of turnips soon after I parachuted into Germany when I thought I was still free! With the potato or turnip there was some watery soup, I have no idea what it was made of, but it tasted awful and that is putting it mildly. As far as I was aware, there was only one cooking facility situated in the centre of the camp operated by prisoners and supervised by Germans.

The sanitary facilities were not quite so bad as on the march, but still they were awful places we were forced to use. The latrines, or bog as they were often called, were long buildings separate from the living accommodation, each with a bench type seating back to the wall with twenty/twenty-four holes very close together, and positioned over a trench. With dysentery being rife in the camp, there was often queues waiting their turn. For some reason there didn't seem to be any means of emptying the trenches mechanically, then after complaining of the stench, dilly carts arrived one night to clean them out.

For several days there was a daily display by a twin jet aircraft, similar to our Meteor, we called it the moral booster for the Germans.

Our moral booster was the daily allied aircraft bombing targets in and around Moosburg and Munich, plus there was action on the ground from the American troops under the command of General Patton, it became obvious they were getting nearer by the hour. Their heavy guns were firing over us, this made us feel uncomfortable being underneath the action. Guns based in a factory then returned fire, but it did not stop the advance of the Americans.

Herr General (Camp Commandant) had us all muster to hear him say as he raised his arms in the air "Today you are my prisoners, tomorrow I shall be yours, Goodbye".

The Americans were brilliant and it was a great day when they arrived on the morning of the 29th April 1945. We were liberated by some of the 14th Armoured Division of General Patton's 3rd Army. Pandemonium broke out when the first tanks smashed through the wire fence. Many of the German guards had already deserted their posts, but some of the 'Goons' were determined to make a stand and continued walking up and down with their dogs. No doubt regretting their decision when eventually they were taken prisoners, the shoe being on the other foot as it were!

What I didn't know at the time, and I'm still not sure it is fact, but I am given to understand that Hitler had given the order for all prisoners to be killed before they could be liberated. It is possible that the German guards saved us from the order being carried out by the dreaded SS troops in conjunction with the Gestapo.

Shortly after midday on the day we were liberated, the American flag was hoisted over Moosburg. Although I had only been in captivity for a short period, it was a sight to behold, but many internees had been in Stalags for two, three and four years, so the American flag flying over Germany brought tears to many eyes. It meant we were all free from the Hitler regime.

The following day American support troops started distributing more rations than we had seen for many a long day. The food was beyond our wildest dreams, the 'Yanks' certainly knew how to eat, even in wartime conditions. There was white bread, that in it self was a luxury, but peaches and cream, doughnuts and meat stew, it was fantastic. Unfortunately for me the food was far too rich and I was violently sick, a condition that lasted for several days.

Two days after we were liberated, Old Blood and Guts, as he was affectionately known, General George S. Patton. Jnr., arrived amid tumultuous cheers. He was obviously moved by the sight of thousands of prisoners looking so gaunt and scraggy, but he and his troops had done a great job in liberating us.

It was not long before we were all loaded onto trucks and moved out of Moosburg with no idea of our destination, but at least we were free. The journey was very revealing as we passed through the German countryside. Houses had great shell holes, the result of the recent advancing Army. None of it was a pretty sight, especially the many dead German soldiers lying where they had been killed, many of them had bare feet having been relieved of their boots by the Americans, so we were told.

Eventually we arrived at a small airfield at Regensburg on the banks of the River Danube, where we had to sleep rather rough, but it was no worse than when we were on the march, the weather was better and, as I said, we were free. Then a group of us were given accommodation in a section of a local hospital, this was real luxury.

Every day we made our way to the airstrip hoping for a plane to take us to Blighty, in the words I believe to be in a song, 'Blighty is the place for me', but the first POW's to be airlifted was hundreds of French. Unbeknown to us at the time, but apparently there was an agreement between General Charles de Gaulle and General Dwight Eisenhower that the French would have priority, for whatever reason.

Eventually our turn came with the arrival of a fleet of USAAF Dakota's that flew us to an airfield at Rheims in France, one step nearer home. It was only a brief stay at Rheims, then I was airlifted by a RAF Lancaster Bomber to RAF Wing in the UK.

Royal Air Force Wing situated 4 miles from Leighton Buzzard in Buckinghamshire, 92 Group Bomber Command, Opened 1941 closed 1958. Total personnel 2,487 including 511 WAAF.

At RAF Wing facilities had been set up where we were stripped, deloused and given fresh clothes as required, at last I was free of my lodgers! However, my feet were still in a ragged and sore condition that made walking difficult.

We were then transported to the railway station, on boarding the train I saw a picture on the wall of the carriage that was of Newark on Trent, my home town, and what a beautiful picture it was. I felt I was going home at last. But our next destination was RAF Padgate

Royal Air Force Station, Padgate, near Warrington, Lancashire. Recruiting centre at the beginning of World War II. On reaching Padgate, we had a shower and were given more fresh clothing. We were also given a talk by a board, (a sort of debriefing exercise) and I was then sent home on leave.

Arriving at Newark on the milk train at five o-clock one morning meant I had to walk from the railway station and knock the family up to gain access to my home. Everyone was soon up to greet me, and what a welcome I received. It really was good to be home amongst a loving family. My blisters had not healed by the time I arrived home, so Jessie, my wife, had to rub cold cream on my feet every night before I could get to sleep, and again in the morning.

Having completed a total of just on 445 hours of flying (257.20 daytime & 187.45 night) and having a relaxed and refreshing six-week leave, I returned to a ground job and was moved around to various places. Then finally at the end of 1945 I was posted to 264 MU at Alconbury, the Station being under the control of the 8th USAAF.

On the 19th March 1945 I was promoted to Flying Officer (F/O), and on the 1st April 1946 I was promoted to Acting Flight Lieutenant. My career in the RAF then ended on the 9th December 1946.

Life was good to me, although I had some unpleasant times, the memory of that horrendous march haunted me. This was something I had to endure, and my therapy when on leave was to cut old clothes into strips and make pegged rugs, which proved to be a most productive thing to do.

My thoughts are often with my crew, Gordon, Bill, Tom and Cyril, one minute we were cocooned in an aeroplane, a sort of a family unit, then in a split second we had parted and I was dropping to earth by parachute. I still shed a tear for my two pals, Bob and Taffy who didn't make it, they certainly deserved better than a grave in a foreign land! Bob and I shared the same billet in the UK, and Bob was an accomplished musician. My lasting thoughts are of Bob and I sitting on our respective beds and Bob playing his clarinet for hours on end. Now when I hear that instrument played, a shiver goes up my spine. My one hope is that Bob and Taffy, and thousands more like them, did not give their lives in vain!

"We Will Remember Them".

Flight. Lieutenant Philip Henry Clews. ex-RAF.

I read this piece of verse at the 'Battle of Britain' service in Boston Stump on Sunday 20th September 1981 and I have treasured it ever since.

Words from Pericles' Funeral Oration over Athenians killed in war B.C. 431. *(Thucydides III, Trans. Rex Warner)*

When you realise the greatness of your city, then reflect that what made her great was men with a spirit of adventure, men who knew their duty, men who were ashamed to fall below a certain standard. If ever they failed in an enterprise, they made up their minds that at any rate the city should not find their courage lacking to her, and they gave her the best contribution they could. They gave her their lives, to her and to all of us; and for their own selves they won praises that never grow old, the most splendid of sepulchres – not the sepulchre in which their bodies are laid, but where their glory remains eternal in men's minds, always there on the right occasion to stir others to speech or to action.

For famous men have the whole earth as their memorial: it is not only the inscriptions on their graves in their own country that mark them out, no, in foreign lands also, not in any visible form but in people's hearts, their memory abides and grows. It is for you to try to be like them. Make up your minds that happiness depends on being free, and freedom depends on being courageous.

S.N.

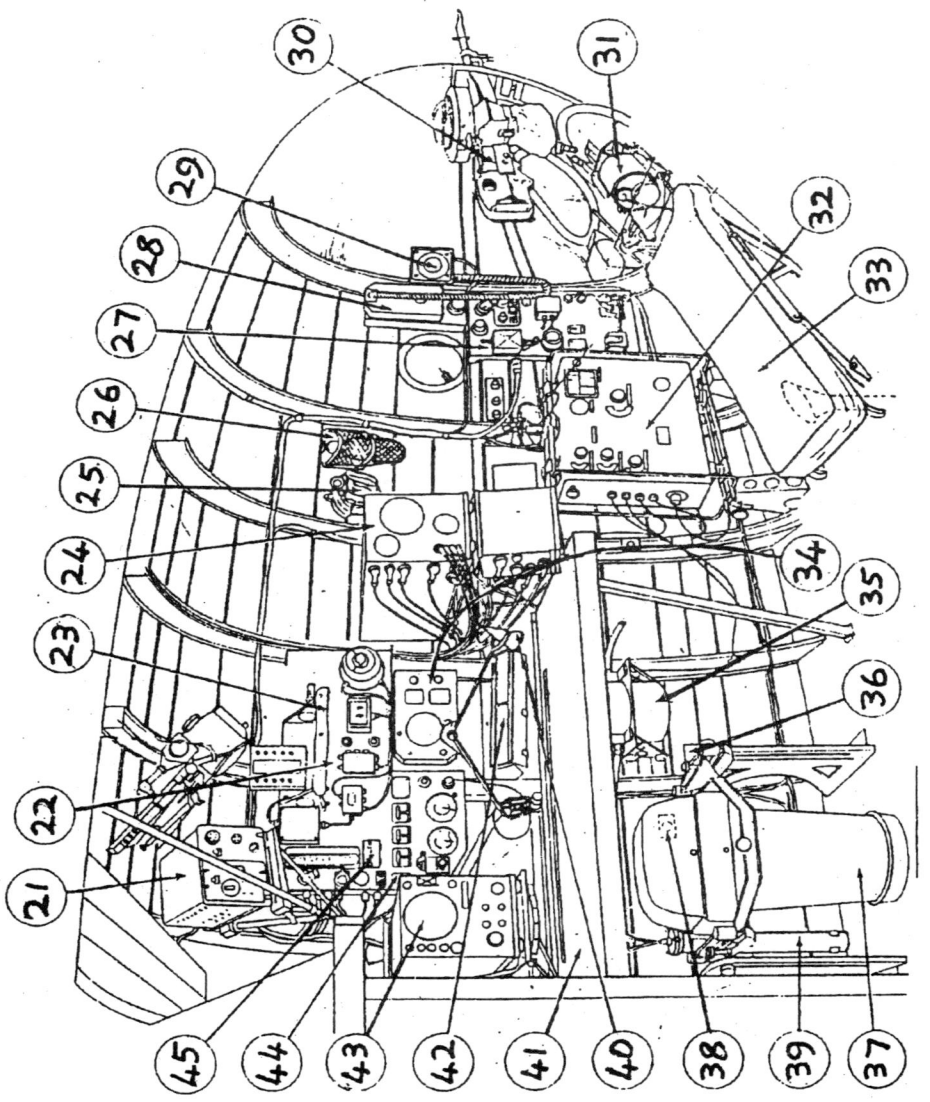

KEY TO DIAGRAM OF NAVIGATOR'S STATION

21 'Gee' Receiver Unit
22 Navigator's Instrument Panel
23 Astrograph Mounting
24 H2S Indicator Unit
25 Signalling Lamp
26 Emergency Oxygen Bottle
27 Port Air Bomber's Panel
28 Oxygen Economiser
29 D.R. Compass Repeater
30 Vickers G.O. Gun
31 Bombsight Sighting Head
32 Mk XIV Bombsight Computer
33 Air Bombers Couch
34 Air Position Indicator
35 Air Mileage Unit (if fitted)
36 Gravity Impact Switches
37 F24 Camera
38 Camera Magazine
39 Air Drier
40 Adjustable Lamp
41 Navigator's Table
42 Navigation Instruments Stowage
43 'Gee' Indicator Units
44 Navigator's Crash Switch
45 Radar Demolition Switches

LAYOUT OF HALIFAX NAVIGATORS STATION

BEYOND THE WIRE.

Walk the compound bomber boy
    And hate its every yard;
The Jerry's clipped your wings old son,
    A Kriegie's life is hard.

Pace along the hard packed mud,
    But not too near barbed wire.
Don't even dream of vaulting,
    You would die from Mauser fire.

Step out nice and brisk then,
    It'll take your mind off food,
And do not mock your favourite 'Goon,
    He's in a filthy mood.

Despair with every step lad,
    No use to yearn for home.
Barbed wire and guards to hold you,
    There's not much chance you'll roam.

Next week a Red Cross parcel,
    If Jerry hands them out.
A bar of chocolate goes down well:
    When you eat next to nowt'.

Tread the dusty compound,
    Forget about that girl.
It's quite a while from now 'till then,
    Did she make your head fair whirl?

There are aircrews from all nations;
    British; Canucks; Yanks;
Aussies; Poles and Kiwis;
    Men of many ranks.

Be thankful you survived son,
   The Reaper passed you by.
But others weren't so lucky
   For thousands had to die.

So fight to keep your chin up,
   And see the long months through.
Remember; when it's over,
   Sweet freedom waits for you.

       © *John R. Walsh 1986.*

JOHNNY BOY

Warm gold this day, so blue the sky
   And proud the blue you wore;
A pilot's brevet on your breast
   Through hostile days of war.

May the times we had be ever bright,
   Your laughter quelled my tears;
Now here I stand at Runnymede,
   My vigil trough the years.

Your name among the thousands
   Etched clear into the stone;
'Twixt other names and many lives
   Though I know but yours alone.

Your memorial stands in tribute
   And I lament with saddened heart;
Do echo grief of other souls,
   Who were, like us, to part.

       © John R. Walsh 1986.

THE HANDLEY PAGE HALIFAX

The Avro Lancaster Bomber has taken pride of place in the 'Battle of Britain Memorial Flight' based at RAF Coningsby in Lincolnshire, of which 7,377 were built. It also has the distinction of being associated with 617 Squadron and the Dambusters.

Working alongside the Lancaster, and also a magnificent and versatile aircraft that is often forgotten, was the Handley Page Halifax of which 6,176 were built. Besides the production by the parent company, London Aircraft Production Group, English Electric, Rootes and Fairey Aviation produced Halifax aircraft. This aircraft operated just over four years during World War II, 1941 to 1945, flying over 75,500 bombing sorties, this was a tremendous contribution to the ending of the Nazis regime.

Perhaps not as elegant as the Lancaster, but the Halifax was one of the heavy four-engine aircraft that did sterling work in varying rolls besides its bombing missions. This included dropping special agents, paratroops and supplies into enemy territory, served as an ambulance, plus its maritime and glider towing activities.

The Handley Page Halifax aircraft was introduced to the RAF in November 1940 and on the 10/11th March 1941 made its first bombing operation of the war, the target was Le Havre. It also has the distinction with the Mosquito, of being the last Bomber Command aircraft to operate a bombing mission against Germany. The target was Kiel on the 2nd May 1945. Unfortunately two Halifax aircraft crashed, they may therefore have the distinction of being the last Bomber Command aircraft to be lost in World War II.

At the end of the war in Europe, several squadrons of Halifax aircraft operated in the Far East conflict against Japan.

The dimensions of a Handley Page Halifax Mk.III aircraft are:
Wing span 104 feet 2 ins.; length 71 feet 7 in.; height 20 ft. 9 ins.

These dimensions are quoted purely for interest:
Lancaster Mk.III.
Wing span 102 feet; length 68 feet 11 ins.; height 19 feet 6 ins.
Short Stirling.
Wing span 99 feet 1 in.; length 87 feet 3 ins.; height 22 feet 0 ins.

578 Royal Air Force Squadron.

578 Squadron excelled itself during the brief period it operated Halifax's at RAF Snaith and Burn in No 4 Group Bomber Command, from January 1944 to April 1945. The Squadron carried out no less than 2,721 sorties, and two of its aircraft each passed the century mark flying a combined total of 209 missions. Unfortunately during this period 55 Halifax's failed to return to RAF Burn, one of those was LK-T which was shot down in Germany in which Philip Clews was a navigator.

Individual awards are not known, apart from the VC presented posthumously to Plt.Off. C.J. Barton, the Pilot of Halifax LK-E on a raid on Nuremberg on the 30th March 1944. Brian J. Rapier tells the story in chapter 8 in his book on the Halifax and Wellington, why this unique award was presented to Plt.Off. Barton.

All the crews of 578 Squadron distinguished themselves on their many raids over enemy territory. The following number of awards were presented to them, 143 DFC's, (Distinguished Flying Cross); and 82 DFM's (Distinguished Flying Medal).

The Squadron Motto was 'Accuracy', and His Majesty King George VI granted the Squadron Crest to 578 in February 1945. The ground crews also earned an accolade in the form of a shield presented to them by the Bristol Aeroplane Company for their outstanding performance of servicing the Bristol Hercules XVI engines. The Bristol Hercules engines powered the Halifax aircraft and the shield is now on display at the Yorkshire Air Museum at Elvington near York.

Sadly 578 Squadron was disbanded in April 1945, but I'm sure Philip Clews was proud to have served as a navigator on such an outstanding aircraft as the Halifax with a Squadron of excellence. .

Stanley Naylor.

"Never in the field of human conflict was so much owed by so many to so few".

Sir Winston Churchill in a speech on the Battle of Britain August 1940.

ABBREVIATIONS & INTERPRETATIONS.

AC2	Aircraftman Second Class.
AC1	Aircraftman First Class.
A/C	Aircraft.
A, B & C'	Alphabetical order of flights in a Squadron.
Aussie - AUS	An Australian.
Bog	Latrine or lavatory.
BBC	British Broadcasting Corporation.
Blighty	British slang for home by service personnel serving abroad, meaning England, and the White Cliffs of Dover is beautiful after serving a spell overseas.
Cannock's	Canadians.
DFC	Distinguished Flying Cross.
DFM	Distinguished Flying Medal.
DR	Direct Reckoning - navigation term.
DR	Dispatch Rider - in transport terms.
DIY	Do-it-yourself.
ETA	Estimated Time of Arrival.
Erk	A person who has just joined the Royal Air Force.
F.I.D.O.	Fog Investigation Dispersal Operation.
Flak	Bursting shells from artillery guns.
Frogs or Froggies	British slang for Frenchmen, derogatory.
F/O	Flying Officer.
Flt. Lt.	Flight Lieutenant.
Flt. Sgt or F/S	Flight Sergeant.
Flying Bomb	Unmanned small explosive-packed guided winged missile powered by a pulse jet. Also known as a 'V1', 'robot bomb' and a 'buzz bomb'.
Gaggle	Group - RAF jargon.
GI	Serviceman in the United States armed forces.
Goons	German Guards in POW camps.
'G' or Gee	A navigational aid, used extensively in World War II.
HCU	Heavy Conversion Unit - upgrading to larger aircraft.
'Hit the Silk'	To leave an aircraft and land safely with a parachute.
'In trouble'	Meaning a girl was pregnant.

Jerry	British slang for German.
Kite	An aircraft.
Kip-down	To sleep.
Klim burner	POW improvised cooker made from used tins.
Kriegie	From the German word Kriegsgefanganer for allied Prisoners of War.
Kraut	British slang for a German - derogatory.
Lilliput	Meaning tiny or small.
LK-V & T	Aircraft markings.
Luft	Luftwaffe, the German Air force World War II.
ME110	German Fighter Aircraft.
MOC	Man of confidence acted as spokesman in POW Camps.
MU	Maintenance Unit.
NAAFI	Navy, Army and Air Force Institutes.
Orbit	To circle - or go round to make a second bombing run.
OTU	Officer Training Unit.
P/O	Pilot Office.
POW	Prisoner of War.
Posting	Being moved from one station to another, or one unit to another. It has nothing whatsoever to do with letters.
Potato Haulms	Dead potato foliage.
PT	Physical Training.
RAF	Royal Air Force.
RCAF	Royal Canadian Air Force.
RAAF	Royal Australian Air Force.
Rtd	Retired.
SAO	Senior American Officer.
Sgt	Sergeant.
T a/c	Total aircraft on raid.
Taffy	Welshmen - could be offensive.
The Reaper	Referring to being killed - or saved - by the hand of God.
u/s	Unservicable.
UK	United Kingdom.
USA	United States of America.

USAAF	United States Army Air Force.
WAAF	Women's Auxiliary Air Force.
'Warm Welcome'	Means there was a lot of flak on a bombing mission.
WOP/AG	Wireless Operator/Air Gunner.
WSW	West South West.
Yanks	Americans.

REMEMBER

Remember us, we would ask you,
   Through dawn and the break of day.
And recall us then with your quiet prayers,
   In the lofting sun's first rays.

Know that we bought your freedom,
   But grieve not hard at the cost.
For better far we pay the highest price,
   Than suffer your future lost.

Remember then, we would ask you,
   Through sunset's last red glow.
And salute us all with the bugle's call,
   For the dawns that we'll never know.

©*John R. Walsh 1985*

Acknowledgements.

I wish to express my thanks and appreciation to Mrs Clews for providing a lot of the information included in this book. A special thanks to her Granddaughter for attempting to decipher her Grandfather's notes that has been a great help in compiling the story. To the authors of the following books, they have helped in corroborating parts of Philip's story, and for providing some details. Also to the Museums, the MOD and anyone else I have contacted who have kindly helped in the completion of this book.

Famous Bombers of the Second World War by William Green.
The Bomber Command War Diaries
                     by Martin Middlebrook and Chris Everitt.
Military Airfields in the British Isles 1939 to 1945 (Omnibus Edition)
                     by Steve Willis and Barry Holliss.
Mr Brian Shields and Mr Bill Napier, Archives, Yorkshire Air
                     Museum, Halifax Way, Elvington, York.
Ms. Nina Burns, Curator, RAF Museum, Hendon, London.
Grp. Capt. Desmond Hollis, RAF, 578 Squadron Association..
Air Historical Branch (RAF), Ministry of Defence, Stanmore,
                     Middlesex.
Halifax and Wellington by Brian J. Rapier and Chaz Bowyer.
The Last Escape by John Nichol and Tony Rennell.
The staff at The Guardian Press (Boston) Ltd, Nelson Way, Boston,

The Royal British Legion Act of Homage

They shall grow not old, as we that are left grow old:
Age shall nor weary them, nor the years condemn.
At the going down of the sun and in the morning,
We will remember them.

Books written and published by Stanley Naylor.

Lincolnshire Country Life beside the Wash 1920's to 1939

This is the history of Fenlanders, true Yellowbellies, who lived, worked and played beside the Wash on the East Coast of the British Isles. This was a farming community where the workers survived without electricity, gas. running water, motor cars, telephones in the homes, and definitely no mobile phones. Bathing was in a tin tub, the bog – toilet – was down the garden path. Cooking was done on a coal fire, in the summer a Valor two/three burner paraffin stove was used. Transport was on shank's pony – walking – bicycle, carriers cart, and trains for long distance travel. Included is the story of the last fishermen/wildfowler's who earned a living in the Northwest corner of the Wash, who were visited by Sir Peter Scott. Dame Sara Swift was born in the area that founded the Royal College of Nursing.

The book is A5 size with a soft cover and has 196 pages. There are over ninety photographs, plus poems relevant to the stories, intriguing village news from that era, and much more.

The Home Front World War II 1939 to 1945.

The Home Front follows on from the above book and is a collection of stories written by various people who lived through World War II. My contribution is small because I was away for five years serving in the RAF Regiment. The stories include the Home Guard, and the Secret Army that was totally separate from the Home Guard. Included also, the Air Sea Rescue; Women's Land Army; Women's Institute; Royal Observer Corps; the Island at War in London's East End; United States Army Air Force; RAF Burns Unit at Rauceby Hospital; an intriguing mail train story; and the meeting years later between a German pilot and the British pilot who shot him down just North of Boston in World War II. There are poems; wartime recipes; advertisements; unique photographs and much more.

There are 214 pages in this A5 size book that has a soft cover. The recommended retail price of both books on this page is £12.95, but is on special offer of £10.00 including post and packing, while present stocks last

Please make cheques payable to Stanley Naylor and post to:
15 Edinburgh Crescent, KIRTON, Boston, Lincolnshire, PE20 1JT.
Tel: 01205 722594.

Memorial Lancaster ED503 'Lest We Forget'.

The committee of the **Sibsey Lancaster Memorial Trust,** consisting of Royal British Legion and Royal Air Forces Association members, are raising some funds to preserve this private memorial for eternity, and to place a wreath of Poppies at its base at the annual service.

The memorial stands proudly in the middle of an arable field where five of its crewmembers are buried. They were killed when their new aircraft crashed in World War II. Not only do we pay tribute to our five comrades laying peacefully beneath this granite stone, but we include the thousands who so gallantly gave their lives for freedom. **"We Will Remember Them".**

This 32 page A5 book is crammed with information regarding the crash, and includes eye witness accounts, poems, the RAF Station where the aircraft was based, plus much more.

Recommended retail price is £4.75, but is on special offer at £4.35 including post and packing. Please make sure cheques are made payable to: **Sibsey Lancaster Memorial Trust,** and post to:
c/o 15 Edinburgh Crescent, KIRTON, Boston, Lincolnshire, PE20 1JT.

My next book is also being produced to raise funds for the
Sibsey Lancaster Memorial Trust
The title:
**Compilation of Poems, Verse
and
Bits & Pieces.**

My very good poetic friend, the late John R. Walsh, wrote thirty poems. Although odd ones have been published in various books including Lancaster at War series, it was his ambition to have them all published in one book. It is my intention to try and fulfil his dream. Included will be some poems of another poetic friend, Victor Cavendish, who wrote a marvellous poem Stand Those Three Towers that refers to Lincoln Cathedral and the county of Lincolnshire.

It is envisaged the book will be in print about three months after this one is published. The estimated cost will be about £1 more than the price of this book